So Cute! Baby Animals
Llamas

By Julia Jaske

Baby llamas like to walk.

Baby llamas like to look.

Baby llamas like to drink.

Baby llamas like to play.

Baby llamas like to sniff.

Baby llamas like to run.

Baby llamas like to climb.

Baby llamas like to smile.

Baby llamas like to stand.

Baby llamas like to spit.

Baby llamas like to chew.

Baby llamas like to rest.

Word List

Baby	play	stand
llamas	sniff	spit
walk	run	chew
look	climb	rest
drink	smile	

60 Words

Baby llamas like to walk.
Baby llamas like to look.
Baby llamas like to drink.
Baby llamas like to play.
Baby llamas like to sniff.
Baby llamas like to run.
Baby llamas like to climb.
Baby llamas like to smile.
Baby llamas like to stand.
Baby llamas like to spit.
Baby llamas like to chew.
Baby llamas like to rest.

Published in the United States of America by Cherry Lake Publishing Group
Ann Arbor, Michigan
www.cherrylakepublishing.com

Book Designer: Melinda Millward

Photo Credits: © Inesmeierfotografie/Shutterstock, cover, 1; © Gretchen Gunda Enger/Shutterstock, 2; © GSPstock/Shutterstock, 3; © Delpixel/Shutterstock, 4; © LouieLea/Shutterstock, 5; © LABETAA Andre/Shutterstock, 6; © Lauren Squire/Shutterstock, 7; © Mark Pitt Images/Shutterstock, 8; © Ved_den/Shutterstock, 9; © Batard Jean MArc/Shutterstock, 10; © Andrew Goodsell/Shutterstock, 11; © Peter Ekvall/Shutterstock, 12; © Nora Yusuf/Shutterstock, 13; © dmitriy_rnd/Adobe Stock, 14

Copyright © 2023 by Cherry Lake Publishing Group
All rights reserved. No part of this book may be reproduced or utilized in any form or by any means without written permission from the publisher.

Cherry Blossom Press is an imprint of Cherry Lake Publishing Group.

Library of Congress Cataloging-in-Publication Data

Names: Jaske, Julia, author.
Title: Llamas / written by Julia Jaske.
Description: Ann Arbor, Michigan : Cherry Lake Publishing, [2022] | Series: So cute! Baby animals
Identifiers: LCCN 2022009902 | ISBN 9781668908846 (paperback) | ISBN 9781668913628 (pdf) | ISBN 9781668912034 (ebook)
Subjects: LCSH: Llamas—Infancy—Juvenile literature.
Classification: LCC QL737.U54 J37 2022 | DDC 599.63/67—dc23/eng/20220331
LC record available at https://lccn.loc.gov/2022009902

Cherry Lake Publishing Group would like to acknowledge the work of the Partnership for 21st Century Learning, a Network of Battelle for Kids. Please visit http://www.battelleforkids.org/networks/p21 for more information.

Printed in the United States of America
Corporate Graphics